21-day Prayer Journal

Prayers for Me Before We

A Husband in the Making

by

Jemece Gasaway, Monica Thompson
& Latoyia R. Williams

Prayers for Me Before We: A Husband in the Making
published by Watersprings Publishing, a division of Watersprings Media House, LLC.
P.O. BOX 1284
Olive Branch, MS 38654
www.waterspringsmedia.com
Contact publisher for bulk orders and permission requests.

Copyrights © 2019 by Jemece Gasaway, Monica Thompson & Latoyia R. Williams

All rights reserved. No part of this publication may be reproduced, distributed, or transmitted in any form or by any means, including photocopying, recording, or other electronic or mechanical methods, without the prior written permission of the publisher, except in the case of brief quotations embodied in critical reviews and certain other noncommercial uses permitted by copyright law.

Scripture quotations credited to NIV are from the Holy Bible, New International Version. Copyright © 1973, 1978, 1984, 2011 by Biblica, Inc. Used by permission. All rights reserved worldwide.

Scripture quotations marked "NKJV" are taken from the New King James Version. Copyright © 1982 by Thomas Nelson, Inc. Used by permission. All rights reserved.

Scripture quotations credited to NASB are from the New American Standard Bible, copyright © 1960, 1962, 1963, 1968, 1971, 1972, 1973, 1975, by the Lockman Foundation. Used by permission.

Printed in the United States of America.

Library of Congress Control Number: 2019915559

ISBN-13: 978-1-948877-36-7

Table of Contents

	Introduction	1
Day One	Faith	3
Day Two	Heart	6
Day Three	Confidence	9
Day Four	Leadership	12
Day Five	Trust	15
Day Six	Friendship	18
Day Seven	Courage	21
Day Eight	Pride	24
Day Nine	Communication	27
Day Ten	Temptation	30
Day Eleven	Submission	33
Day Twelve	Influence	36
Day Thirteen	Patience	39
Day Fourteen	Forgiveness	42
Day Fifteen	Purpose	45
Day Sixteen	Discernment	48
Day Seventeen	Mental Health	51
Day Eighteen	Wisdom	54
Day Nineteen	Stewardship	57
Day Twenty	Physical Health	60
Day Twenty-One	Grace	63
	About The Authors	66

Prayers for Me Before We

Introduction

Hey Fellas! We are excited that you have picked up this book! This 21-day prayer journal is written to provide you an opportunity to pray about, and reflect on where you are when it comes to the topics of faith, courage, friendships, submission, mental health and much more.

Whether you hope to marry a woman who loves sports, cooking, cleaning, and wants sex three times a day; this book will give you a realistic look at where you are in your relationship with God, yourself, and others. You have the chance to answer questions about yourself that you may not have thought of, and pray to God about what to do with those answers. It will allow you to take an honest look at different areas in your life that can shape and test your character and belief system in all types of relationships.

Me Before We will help you determine some of the areas you need to work on before even entering a relationship, while dating/engaged and even in marriage. Being whole and self-aware at any time in your life is a blessing. To have an opportunity to work on that with guidance and purpose is not only healthy but sure to prove helpful as well.

Through prayer, reflection, and a willingness to be open and honest with yourself and God, this book is sure to be a blessing to you and for all of those that you have a relationship with, present and future.

As you develop your own prayers, the questions will align with the mnemonic, P.R.A.Y., which highlights four key areas of prayer.

P – Praise: Offer praises to God, thank Him for who He is and what He has done

R – Repent: Confess your sins and shortcomings to God

A – Ask: Make your requests and needs known to God

Y – Yield: Yield to His will, listen to His voice, and seek His direction, be obedient

Throughout our books you will see what we refer to as *Relationship Road Work Signs*. These signs are meant as instructional tools to provide guidance for you to get the most out of your experience as you read and apply what you learn.

Men Working - Work

This sign alerts you to the start of your journey in this book. Prepare your heart and mind to be open to everything that comes next.

Rest Area - Reflect

When you see this sign give thought to what God has revealed to you through your answers to the questions. Meditate on your prayer to Him and where He is leading you.

Yield - Proceed with Caution

This sign alerts you to the end of this book, but the beginning of the next step in your journey. Take what you've learned and heard from God, and submit to it!

Again, we are thrilled about your 21-day journey through this book, as well as your lifelong journey in relationships! We look forward to the healing and wholeness prayer will bring about!

DAY ONE

Faith

"Now faith is confidence in what we hope for and assurance about what we do not see"
Hebrews 11:1 NIV

Lord, I praise You, for You deserve the highest praise! I know it is impossible to please You if I don't have faith. So, I come, asking that You increase my faith in You and in my abilities granted through You. Remove all doubts and fears that are placed upon me from day to day by myself and the enemy. Help me to remember that I can do all things through You, You are the one who provides me with strength. Mold me into a man that not only talks faith but puts faith into action. Lord, I want to be a witness for You. I want others to be able to look at me and see what it looks like to live and walk in faith, basing my decisions on Your word and promises, regardless of what is and is not visible. Lord, as I prepare for marriage, help me to embrace the power of faith; allowing myself to be led by it and not by my own understanding, self-will or self-reliance.

In Jesus' name I pray, Amen!

What blessings have you seen come to pass in your life as you have put your faith in God? (Praise)

_____
_____
_____
_____

In what ways do you think that you've sinned or stumbled by not putting your faith in God? (Repent)

_____
_____
_____
_____

What are some specific areas in your life that you need to put your faith in God into action? (Ask)

_____
_____
_____
_____

In what ways do you need to yield to His will in order to demonstrate your faith in Him? (Yield)

_____
_____
_____
_____

Prayers for Me Before We

Write your prayer about faith in God.

DAY TWO

"Above all else, guard your heart, for everything you do flows from it."
Proverbs 4:23 NIV

Heavenly Father, I adore and praise You for who You are. Thank You for Your goodness and thank You for displaying the true meaning of a pure heart. Forgive me Lord for doing the exact opposite of Your word – not guarding what I allow to enter my heart and therefore, allowing things unholy to flow from it. I come to You today asking for a changed and humbled heart. Please help me to be more aware of what messages and spirits I surround myself with daily and allow to permeate my soul. Please remove anything from my heart that is not of You and will keep me from experiencing and displaying the fruits of Your Holy Spirit. Lord, as I await my wife, provide me with strength and patience as You work on me and make me more suitable for marriage. I pray that my eyes are open and that I am receptive to things that You place before me that I need to work on and do differently. As I turn more toward You Lord, I ask that I develop a heart that will always seek and initiate peace and reconciliation.

In Jesus' name I pray, Amen!

What blessings have you seen come to pass in your life when you've acted with a pure heart? (Praise)

_____
_____
_____
_____

Can you identify times when you've sinned as a result of your heart not being in the right place? (Repent)

_____
_____
_____
_____

What are some specific areas in your life that you need God to change your heart? (Ask)

_____
_____
_____
_____

In what ways do you need to yield to His will to demonstrate a heart committed to Him? (Yield)

_____
_____
_____
_____

A Husband in the Making

Write your prayer about your heart condition.

DAY THREE

Confidence

"Let us then approach God's throne of grace with confidence, so that we may receive mercy and find grace to help us in our time of need."
Hebrews 4:16

Father God, Thank You. Thank You for life, thank You for hope. Thank You Jesus for dying on the cross for us so that we may have everlasting life. Father, please forgive me of my lack of assurance in You and myself. Things are not always ideal in my life. I've allowed financial issues, employment issues, relationship issues, and the fact that I have to prove myself daily to the world to burden me and to bring uncertainty to my soul. God, I pray that You remove my insecurities and self-doubt. As I know these things are not of You. Bless me with wisdom and knowledge. Elevate my confidence as You help me to realize my identity and righteous place in You. Help me to identify satan's schemes to steal, kill, and destroy my confidence and faith in You and myself. As I prepare to lead in marriage, bless me with vision; reveal Your will and purpose for my life so that I can determine and follow your path, I ask that you lead me through scripture and supportive community. Lord I ask that you please remove worry, doubt, fear, and shame from my heart while replacing it with Your Spirit of faith, love, and confidence.

In Jesus' Name I pray, Amen!

What blessings have you seen come to pass in your life as you have put your confidence in God? (Praise)

_____
_____
_____
_____

In what ways do you think that you've sinned or stumbled by not putting your confidence in God? (Repent)

_____
_____
_____
_____

What are some specific areas in your life that you need to put your confidence in God into action? (Ask)

_____
_____
_____
_____

In what ways do you need to yield to His will to demonstrate confidence in Him? (Yield)

_____
_____
_____
_____

Prayers for Me Before We

Write your prayer about confidence in God.

DAY FOUR

Leadership

"But the fruit of the Spirit is love, joy, peace, forbearance, kindness, goodness, faithfulness, gentleness and self-control. Against such things there is no law."
Galatians 5:22-23

Father, I confess that I have been a poor leader. I was taught that leadership was about keeping it "real", making the tough decisions, and most importantly, the money. Then I read Galatians 5:22-23 and realized that I don't possess any of those attributes in my leading. In all honesty Father there is a voice always telling me that if I demonstrate these attributes then I will be looked at as weak and soft somehow, please forgive me. I know that Christ was not weak but strong. Please teach me to take responsibility whether anyone else does or not. Teach me not to be passive. Show me how to lead without words. Please teach me how to exercise these fruits in my life before my future spouse so that I may truly be the leader that You are pleased with.

In Jesus' Name I pray, Amen!

What blessings have you seen come to pass in your life as you have shown great leadership? (Praise)

_____
_____
_____
_____

In what ways do you think that you've struggled to follow God and the leadership of those He's placed in your life? (Repent)

_____
_____
_____
_____

What are some specific areas in your life you need to listen to God's leading, and the instruction of others He has placed in your life to lead you? (Ask)

_____
_____
_____
_____

How can your unwillingness to follow God and other leadership, impact your relationship with your future spouse? (Yield)

_____
_____
_____
_____

A Husband in the Making

Write your prayer about being led by God and others.

DAY FIVE

Trust

"Commit your way to the LORD, Trust also in Him, And He shall bring it to pass."
Psalms 37:5 NKJV

More than anything God allow me to faithfully trust You and Your word concerning my life. I pray that trust trumps fear in every situation that I find myself facing so that my life is lived with God confidence and not disrupted by the insecurities of myself and others. My desire is to be trustworthy and safe for the woman You place in my life as a wife. I want her to be able to lean on me as I lean on You knowing that You have a plan and it is not to harm us but to give us hope and a future. I bless You for all that You've already done in my life, showing me that there is no failure in You or Your word. I am grateful for the trust that You've shown in me by the life-changing redemptive power of Your Son Jesus in my life. God, I praise You in advance for the road ahead. May my faith conquer my reservations, for Your glory!

In Jesus' Name I pray, Amen!

What blessings have you seen come to pass in your life as you have put your trust in God? (Praise)

_____
_____
_____
_____

In what ways do you think that you've sinned or stumbled by not putting your trust in God? (Repent)

_____
_____
_____
_____

What are some specific areas in your life that you need to put your trust in God into action? (Ask)

_____
_____
_____
_____

In what ways do you need to yield to His will to demonstrate trust in Him? (Yield)

_____
_____
_____
_____

Write your prayer about trusting God.

DAY SIX

Friendship

"A man who has friends must himself be friendly, But there is a friend who sticks closer than a brother."
Proverbs 18:24 NKJV

God I thank You for the desire to listen and be fed by those who have my best interests at heart. I pray now God that You surround me with those that You have sent to encourage, strengthen and provide me with sound wisdom during this time of waiting. In the midst of the courting process, allow others to speak from sight where I have blinders on, and thereby guide me so that I don't fall. Send those who have been where I am and are now on the other side. Those who don't mind walking with me during this part of my journey, sharing their experiences and prayerfully providing insight into mine. Open up my ears so that I may hear and increase in understanding. As I ultimately sit under Your counsel God please help me grow in understanding and apply the knowledge that comes from You.

In Jesus' Name I pray, Amen!

Prayers for Me Before We

What blessings have you seen come to pass through the friends in your life? (Praise)

_____
_____
_____
_____

In what ways do you think that you've struggled to choose the right friendships? (Repent)

_____
_____
_____
_____

What friendships do you have in your life that you know aren't godly? (Ask)

_____
_____
_____
_____

In what ways do you need to yield to His will regarding your current friendships? (Yield)

_____
_____
_____
_____

A Husband in the Making

Write your prayer about godly friendships.

DAY SEVEN

Courage

"Watch, stand fast in the faith, be brave, be strong."
I Corinthians 16:13 NKJV

Lord, although faint at times, my heart is so grateful for Your love and sacrifice for me. Please help me not to fear. I know Your word says that You have not given me a spirit of fear, but there are times that I lack the courage to act on Your word due to what I see. Teach me to see things as You see them. When the facts don't line up please settle my Spirit in You that I may display the courage needed for my faith to please You. I do believe that You are ever present so please answer me when I'm weak that my Spirit may be renewed within. Bless me with courage of David so my future family can experience a man after Your own heart. I'm not asking for things to be easy since they weren't for Your Son, just that I am heard when I call out. Thank You for hearing my prayers always. I can feel Your love inside of me at work. Thank You for being my God in whom I can trust with all of me.

In Jesus' Name I pray, Amen!

What blessings have you seen come to pass in your life when you've exhibited courage? (Praise)

_____
_____
_____
_____

In what ways do you think that you've sinned by not showing courage? (Repent)

_____
_____
_____
_____

What are some specific areas in your life right now that you know you need to show courage? (Ask)

_____
_____
_____
_____

In what ways do you need to yield to His will to demonstrate courage? (Yield)

_____
_____
_____
_____

Write your prayer about courage in God.

DAY EIGHT

Pride

"Pride goes before destruction, And a haughty spirit before stumbling."
Proverbs 16:18 NASB

Dear God, Thank You for being everything I will ever need. Thank You for being perfect in everything. Thank you for being majestic and all knowing. God, You've blessed me to achieve dreams greater than I could ever imagine and I thank You. You've blessed me with a fulfilling career, financial stability, and a loving family. At times, I forget those blessings are from You. Sometimes, I think my accolades at work are due to my own efforts and I forget to praise You for leading me. God, for displaying arrogance I beg You for forgiveness. I know I cannot exist in this world without You. God, I don't want to be prideful or arrogant anymore. When I want to rely on my abilities, remind me to seek You first. When I want to brag about my accomplishments, remind me to season my sentences with adoration for You and thanksgiving for the talents You've given me. When I am boastful about places I've gone or things I have, allow me to recall those around me who don't have or who have had and lost. God, when I lose myself in my job or my belongings, refocus my thoughts on the permanence that rests with You.

In Jesus' Name I pray, Amen!

What blessings have you seen come to pass in your life when you displayed humility over pride? (Praise)

_____
_____
_____
_____

In what ways do you know that you've sinned or stumbled by being prideful in the past? (Repent)

_____
_____
_____
_____

What are some specific areas in your life that you need to ask God to remove pride? (Ask)

_____
_____
_____
_____

In what ways do you need to yield to His will regarding your pride? (Yield)

_____
_____
_____
_____

A Husband in the Making

Write your prayer about pride.

REST AREA →

DAY NINE

Communication

"A soft answer turns away wrath, But a harsh word stirs up anger."
Proverbs 15:1 NKJV

Heavenly Father, I pray that You place a guard over my heart and my lips, for out of the heart the mouth speaks, and I want to speak words that edify the hearer and magnify Your name. Allow the meditation of my heart to be acceptable in Your sight so that I might know when and how to speak to those that I come into contact with throughout my days. I desire to be a man that washes his woman in the word so that she is honored and aware that she is a special gift to me from You. Lord I want to not only say the right things in the right way, but I want to be able to hear clearly and without being guarded or defensive. My desire is to be able to communicate Your love and patience for me as I communicate with others. I pray You deal with my anger, bitterness and intolerance so that I am sober-minded and ready to speak peace into the hearers life through grace and patience.

In Jesus' Name I pray, Amen!

What blessings have you seen come to pass in your life as you have communicated with God before moving forth in action? (Praise)

_____

_____

_____

_____

In what ways do you think that you've sinned or stumbled by not communicating with God first? (Repent)

_____

_____

_____

_____

What are some specific areas in your life right now that you know you need to communicate with God about? (Ask)

_____

_____

_____

_____

In what ways do you need to yield to His will regarding your communication? (Yield)

_____

_____

_____

_____

Prayers for Me Before We

Write your prayer about how you communicate with God and others.

DAY TEN

Temptation

"No temptation has overtaken you except such as is common to man; but God is faithful, who will not allow you to be tempted beyond what you are able, but with the temptation will also make the way of escape, that you may be able to bear it."
I Corinthians 10:13 NKJV

God, I come to you with a heart of repentance, I know that I have not done all that I know to do according to Your word and Your will for me. I find myself doing those things that I shouldn't and not doing the things that I should. Lord please surround me with people who mean me good and not evil. Allow my eyes to be wide open to the tricks of the enemy but not ignorant of my own lustful desires and triggers. My past is in the past and I know that You're able to make all things brand new. God whether it be the common distractions of women, money or power, please allow me to stay focused and in line with where You are guiding so that I don't find myself in situations that I am unable to see the way of escape and be freed.

In Jesus' Name I pray, Amen!

What blessings have you seen come to pass in your life when you've resisted temptation of any kind? (Praise)

_____
_____
_____
_____

In what ways have you sinned or stumbled by not resisting temptation? (Repent)

_____
_____
_____
_____

What are some specific areas in your life that you are tempted in, and you need to ask God to help you? (Ask)

_____
_____
_____
_____

In what ways do you need to yield to His will regarding temptation of your flesh? (Yield)

_____
_____
_____
_____

A Husband in the Making

Write your prayer about temptation.

DAY ELEVEN

Submission

"Submit to one another out of reverence for Christ"
Ephesians 5:21 NIV

God, You are Holy, Magnificent and Worthy of all praise! Lord please allow me to learn submission in every way and from everyone you see fit. I repent as I know that I have gone off on my own so many times and have not submitted to Your will or to those who have the rule over me. In my past I've behaved in ways that I am not proud of, doing things that could have been avoided had I just listened and obeyed. God as You train me up as the man, future husband and father You would have me to be I pray that my example of submission trickles down to those that I am responsible for. I want to show my future wife what it looks like to be fully submitted to Christ and her. Thank You Lord for Your patience and loving kindness, I will humbly await Your guidance so that I can walk in Your perfect will for my life.

In Jesus' Name I pray, Amen!

What blessings have you seen come to pass when you've been submissive? (Praise)

_____
_____
_____
_____

In what ways do you think that you've sinned or struggled by not submitting to God or those who have the rule over you (parents, boss, etc.)? (Repent)

_____
_____
_____
_____

Who are some specific people in your life that you are not submitted to, and you need to ask God to help you to do so? (Ask)

_____
_____
_____
_____

In what ways do you need to yield to His will to demonstrate submission to Him and to your future spouse? (Yield)

_____
_____
_____

Write your prayer about submission.

DAY TWELVE

Influence

"You are the light of the world. A town built on a hill cannot be hidden. Neither do people light a lamp and put it under a bowl. Instead they put it on its stand, and it gives light to everyone in the house."
Matthew 5:14-15 NIV

Father God, You are a light that shines bright wherever there is darkness, in this world and in my life! I bless You for Your light has changed me from the inside out. I repent for the times that I have not broadcasted Your light and been an example and a light for others. I desire to be able to illuminate the minds and lives of others by living according to how You want me to live. God I pray that with Your power and grace I am able to encourage, support, strengthen and enlighten those that You place into my life, be it my future wife, kids, extended family, friends and co-workers. I want my actions and my speech to line up with Your word in such a way that the evidence of You living through me is apparent to all that I come into contact with. I hope to be all that You have called me to be. And when I fall short Lord I pray that You restore me in such a way that it strengthens my testimony and brings glory to Your name!

In Jesus' Name I pray, Amen!

What blessings have you seen come to pass in your life as you have been an influence to others? (Praise)

_____
_____
_____
_____

In what ways do you think that you've sinned or stumbled by not exercising your ability to influence someone or a situation? (Repent)

_____
_____
_____
_____

Who are some people in your life that you know you need to influence? (Ask)

_____
_____
_____
_____

In what ways do you need to yield to His will regarding those you have influence over, as well as those who have influence over you? (Yield)

_____
_____
_____
_____

A Husband in the Making

Write your prayer about your sphere of influence.

DAY THIRTEEN

Patience

"Better a patient person than a warrior, one with self-control than one who takes a city."
Proverbs 16:32 NIV

Lord, I magnify You today, I lift Your holy name. I praise You not only for what You do, but for who You are and Your gift of Salvation. Lord, please help me to break free from the worldly ways of a hurried pace, wanting all things and all answers instantly. Please forgive me for falling short of displaying grace, patience, and self-control toward others, myself, and even You O' Lord. Teach me to trust Your timing. Give me the perseverance to stand strong while I await Your instruction. I need Your wisdom and direction. Grant me to be a man of patience as You equip me to thrive in healthy relationships. Help me to discern Your voice regarding Your will for my life in all areas, including marriage. In addition, please bless me with Your peace, so that I may bless others with a calm and enduring spirit, being slow to anger, always displaying your love and patience.

In Jesus' Name I pray, Amen!

What blessings have you seen come to pass in your life as you have been patient and waited on God? (Praise)

___

In what ways do you think that you've sinned or stumbled by not being patient with God? (Repent)

___

What are some specific areas in your life that you need to be patient and trust God? (Ask)

___

In what ways do you need to yield to His will to demonstrate patience? (Yield)

___

Prayers for Me Before We

Write your prayer about your ability to be patient.

DAY FOURTEEN

Forgiveness

"Bearing with one another, and forgiving each other, whoever has a complaint against anyone; just as the Lord forgave you, so also should you."
Colossians 3:13 NASB

God, thank You for being my Deliverer and my Defense. Thank You for sending Jesus to be my salvation. Each day I wake up, You give me another chance and I thank You. God, I don't always give other people a second or third chance. I often cut them out of my life because it is easier to abandon the relationship than to deal with them or to try to heal the hurt. God I know You want me to be reconciled to anyone where the relationship has been broken. Your Son died for my sins and I know that I have no excuse not to forgive others but at times I still struggle to forgive. Lord, how can I struggle to forgive what is probably a minor offense in light of everything You've done for me? God, please forgive me. I want to forgive them. Forgive me for hurting Your children and others, and please heal our relationships.

In Jesus' Name I pray, Amen!

What blessings have you seen come to pass in your life as you have been forgiving of others and yourself? (Praise)

_____
_____
_____

In what ways do you think that you've sinned or stumbled by not forgiving myself or someone else? (Repent)

_____
_____
_____

What are some specific areas in your life that you need to forgive others or yourself? (Ask)

_____
_____
_____

In what ways do you need to yield to His will to demonstrate forgiveness toward yourself and others? (Yield)

_____
_____
_____

A Husband in the Making

Write your prayer about forgiveness.

DAY FIFTEEN

Purpose

"Many are the plans in a person's heart, but it is the Lord's purpose that prevails."
Proverbs 19:21 NASB

God, thank You for being the Amazing Creator of all things! Thank You for always being right. You know more than I could ever know and Your will and Your way is what's best for me. You've created me for a purpose and while I may not know the purposes yet, I pray that You open my eyes to see. God, I know I can find enjoyment in my career and in spending time with special people but without knowing Your purpose for my life, it will all be useless. I trust You will guide me and close the doors not meant for me and to open the doors You've destined for me. Give me the courage to go through doors even when I'm uncertain of what is on the other side. When I want to give up, I pray You refresh me and encourage me. God, please be gentle with me when I begin to stray off the path You've designed for me. I want to be pleasing to You and I pray that my life is. Thank you for directing my steps God. You know what's best.

In Jesus' Name I pray, Amen!

What blessings have you seen come to pass in your life as you have acted in your purpose? (Praise)

_____
_____
_____
_____

In what ways do you think that you've sinned or stumbled by not acting in your purpose? (Repent)

_____
_____
_____
_____

What are some specific areas in your life that you need to act on purpose? (Ask)

_____
_____
_____
_____

In what ways do you need to yield to His will to live out the purpose He has for your life? (Yield)

_____
_____
_____
_____

Write your prayer about your purpose.

DAY SIXTEEN

Discernment

"Teach me good discernment and knowledge, For I believe in Your commandments."
Psalms 119:66 NASB

God thank You for being trustworthy, my reward, and my Helper. Thank you for giving me another day to have similar and new experiences. God, You know all things so please deepen my mind with Your wisdom. Each day I encounter new situations and I have to decide the best way to respond. Most days, I doubt my abilities and my knowledge and at times, I'm paralyzed from making any decisions. God forgive me for allowing fear to control me. God, I don't want to let You down. You know everything so please help me make the right decisions. Allow me to see the lessons in my previous decisions and guide me to make better decisions. As I spend more time with You and in Your word, give me the wisdom to respond with grace, love, and patience to the people I interact with daily.

In Jesus' Name I pray, Amen!

Prayers for Me Before We

What blessings have you seen come to pass in your life as you have been discerning and listened to the Holy Spirit lead you? (Praise)

_____

_____

_____

_____

In what ways do you think that you've sinned or stumbled by not heeding to the voice of God? (Repent)

_____

_____

_____

_____

What are some specific areas in your life that you've heard and know what to do, but have not acted on it? (Ask)

_____

_____

_____

_____

In what ways do you need to yield to God's will in order to be able to discern His voice and act upon it? (Yield)

_____

_____

_____

_____

A Husband in the Making

Write your prayer about discerning the voice of God.

DAY SEVENTEEN

Mental Health

"Cast all your anxiety on him because he cares for you."
1 Peter 5:7 NIV

Lord, You are Holy! You are loving! You are gracious! Thank You for knowing our needs and wants before we ask. I pray for my mental and emotional wellbeing. As a man, we are shown repeated examples of suppressing our feelings and distracting ourselves with temporal activities. God, I want to be different but I'm unsure of how 'different' may look. Please give me the fortitude to sit with uncomfortable feelings and past mistakes until I'm able to reflect and understand myself or my feelings, give me the courage to ask for help. Break down the walls I've erected to protect myself from further pain or the guilt of the past. I take responsibility for the mistakes I've made; teach me who I am in You. God, don't allow me to isolate myself and give in to the thoughts that I am the only man experiencing these challenges in life. I don't want to rely on my own strength when You desire that I trust You. So give me the determination to do what I can and to leave room for You to be Lord of my life. Thank You for showing me Your strength in my weakness and Your grace in the midst of life's challenges. You're a generous God!

In Jesus' Name I pray, Amen!

What blessings have you seen come to pass in your life when you know you've acted without stress or worry? (Praise)

_____
_____
_____
_____

In what ways do you think that you've sinned or stumbled by doing things when you've been exhausted or not in your "right mind"? (Repent)

_____
_____
_____
_____

What are some specific areas in your life that you need to clear your head and ask for guidance and clarity from God? (Ask)

_____
_____
_____
_____

In what ways do you need to yield to His will to better take care of yourself mentally? (Yield)

_____
_____
_____
_____

Write your prayer about your mental health.

DAY EIGHTEEN

"Know that wisdom is thus for your soul; If you find it, then there will be a future, And your hope will not be cut off."
Proverbs 24:14 NASB

God, You are all knowing and You are my Lamp. Thank You for lighting the paths that I should take in this life. Thank You for enough direction to depend on You and only enough so I don't forget that You are God. It is easy for me as a man to believe I know all the answers but I know I don't. God, I know that having authentic relationships is key to growing in You so I ask that you surround me with other men who are courageous enough to admit they don't know all the answers either and don't try to live their lives as if they do. God I pray that You give me peace when I don't know and give me the wisdom to seek out guidance from others who may have more knowledge and experience than I do. I pray that You forgive me when I've depended on myself instead of turning to You for guidance. Thank You for keeping me humble God, I pray that You are pleased.

In Jesus' Name I pray, Amen!

What blessings have you seen come to pass in your life when you know you've used wisdom in making decisions? (Praise)

_____
_____
_____
_____

In what ways do you think that you've sinned or stumbled by doing things you know weren't wise? (Repent)

_____
_____
_____
_____

What are some specific areas in your life that you need to ask for wisdom from God? (Ask)

_____
_____
_____
_____

In what ways do you need to yield to His will in order to gain wisdom? (Yield)

_____
_____
_____
_____

A Husband in the Making

Write your prayer about wisdom from God.

DAY NINETEEN

Stewardship

"The rich rules over the poor, And the borrower becomes the lender's slave."
Proverbs 22:7 NASB

God, You are Creator and Ruler over everything! You have given me the financial means to travel the world and to buy things I never imagined. Thank you for allowing me to be born at this time and to experience pleasurable times in this life. You've called me to be a good financial steward and most of the time I try to manage Your resources Your way but not always. God, forgive me when I hoarded money and didn't give when You nudged me. Forgive me when I didn't consider Your people before focusing on myself. At other times, I've spent money carelessly and I don't remember the things I've wasted money on. Forgive me when I didn't consider Your ways or Your purpose for allowing me to manage the money You've given me. God, please forgive me when I think this life is all about my happiness. Forgive me for allowing my desires to control me and my financial actions instead of delaying or denying my gratification. God, I want to be pleasing to You. I want to yield my will to Your will financially. I want Your purpose to be my purpose. I want to be the feet You use to reach Your people, please use me God.

In Jesus' Name I pray, Amen!

What blessings have you seen come to pass in your life when you know you've stewarded your finances wisely? (Praise)

_____
_____
_____
_____

In what ways do you think that you've sinned or stumbled by being wasteful or greedy with your finances? (Repent)

_____
_____
_____
_____

What are some specific areas in your life that you need to hear from God concerning purchases you've made or are thinking about making? (Ask)

_____
_____
_____
_____

In what ways do you need to yield to His will to ensure good stewardship of your finances? (Yield)

_____
_____
_____
_____

Write your prayer about financial stewardship.

A Husband in the Making

DAY TWENTY

Physical Health

"Dear friend, I pray that you may enjoy good health and that all may go well with you, even as your soul is getting along well."
3 John 1:2 NIV

Gracious God, I come to You thanking You for the fact that I am still alive today! God I have not always taken care of my physical body, the temple that You have given me, the temple in which Your Spirit resides. I have been neglectful, harmful and outright abusive toward my physical self throughout my lifetime. With Your guidance and wisdom I desire to treat my body as the temple You have deemed it to be. I pray that You show me how to care for my physical self so that I am not only healthy and strong on the inside, but the outside as well. I never want to become vain or conceited about my outward appearance, but I also don't want to be neglectful or harmful to it either. I want to live a quality life with the wife and children that You will bless me with in the future. I want to be a living example of healthy habits and good choices as it pertains to not only my spiritual disciplines but my physical ones as well. Lord, You know me better than I know myself, I pray that I exercise in and with wisdom. Teach when to say no to things that I need to say no to and yes to those things I need to say yes to. I desire to live a long, full life for Your glory!

In Jesus' Name I pray, Amen!

What blessings have you seen come to pass in your life when you know you've been in shape physically? (Praise)

_____
_____
_____
_____

In what ways do you think that you've sinned or stumbled by doing things or eating things you know weren't wise? (Repent)

_____
_____
_____
_____

What are some specific areas of your physical self that you know are unhealthy? (Ask)

_____
_____
_____
_____

In what ways do you need to yield to His will to take better care of yourself physically? (Yield)

_____
_____
_____
_____

A Husband in the Making

Write your prayer about physical health.

DAY TWENTY-ONE

Grace

"For it is by grace you have been saved, through faith—and this is not from yourselves, it is the gift of God— not by works, so that no one can boast."
Ephesians 2:8-9 NIV

Lord, You are amazing! Your grace is always present, thank You! Without Your grace I do not know where I would be. I confess Lord, I am slow to grace. I struggle with extending this attribute to others, especially those who don't say sorry or show that they're deserving of it. I tend to hold it as if it were something that is optional, something that in my flesh that I have the capacity to give. I know that any grace that I give to others or even myself comes from You Lord and Your grace is sufficient in all things. Lord help me to show people grace in spite of my feelings simply because of the grace that You're showing me. When I am in a relationship with the one You have made for me I pray that I remember that grace isn't optional as a christian leader in my household. I desire to follow Your example in the area of extending grace to others with the mindset that they do not know what they are doing just as You do for me daily.

In Jesus' Name I pray, Amen!

What blessings have you seen come to pass in your life when you've extended grace to someone or when someone has extended grace toward you? (Praise)

_____
_____
_____
_____

In what ways do you think that you've sinned or stumbled by not being gracious? (Repent)

_____
_____
_____
_____

What are some specific areas in your life that you need to be more gracious toward others and yourself? (Ask)

_____
_____
_____
_____

In what ways do you need to yield to His will in order to extend grace to others? (Yield)

_____
_____
_____
_____

PRAYERS FOR ME BEFORE We

Write your prayer about the Grace of God.

A Husband in the Making

About the Authors

Me Before We was written by a trio of married, professional Christian women with influence and guidance from their husbands, all who have a heart for walking with singles that desire to marry one day. With over 45 years of marital experience between them, these women know the importance of praying through all seasons of life.

Other books available by Relationship Road Work

Prayers For Me Before We – A Wife in the Making
Road To We – Couples Guide
Road To We – Small Group Curriculm

Follow us @Rel8nshproadwrk on
Facebook, Instagram, and Twitter

Email us at - info@relationshiproadwork.com
website: www.relationshiproadwork.com

www.ingramcontent.com/pod-product-compliance
Lightning Source LLC
Chambersburg PA
CBHW052207110526
44591CB00012B/2107